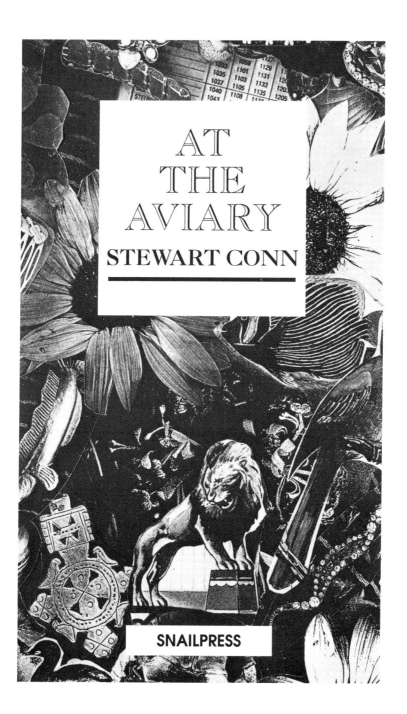

AT
THE
AVIARY

STEWART CONN

SNAILPRESS

SNAILPRESS
30 Firfield Road, Plumstead 7800, South Africa
UK distribution: Crane River, 48 Moor Mead Road,
St Margaret, Middlesex TW1 1JS

A number of these poems have appeared, although not always
in their present form, in *Cencrastus, New Contrast, Slugnews, The
End of a Regime?* (Aberdeen University Press) and *Upstream.*

© S Conn 1995
First published 1995
ISBN 1-874923-21-3

Cover collage by Julia Rosa Clark
Cover design and typesetting by User Friendly, Cape Town
Printed and bound by Interpak, Pietermaritzburg

INTRODUCTION

My first visit to Southern Africa was in 1984, on a Thyne travel scholarship awarded by the English-Speaking Union. For two months Johannesburg was a hub for encounters as far afield as Durban, Cape Town and Gaborone. The experience was in many ways daunting, and poems did not come easily. Nor do they pretend to do more than subjectively touch the outer rim of the land I saw. In the main I suppose, they try to preserve and shape some of the incident and detail which impinged on me. I hope some pattern may be detectable – to outsiders like myself – and to those on whose more profound experience and involvement my observations marginally (and I hope not too presumptuously) encroach.

In 1993 I was invited to be the overseas judge for the Amstel South African National Playwriting Competition. Again city based, I was enabled to do much of the required reading in the bush with the Theatre for Africa Company. Shortly after "Peace Day" my stay was rounded off by a fleeting glimpse of Botswana's magical – and threatened – Okavango Delta. The challenge this time was to capture and celebrate primarily, and more spontaneously, the dazzling beauty and mystery of the bush and the Delta itself. But I like to feel there are shared undercurrents between the two visits – each in its way transforming.

The poems do not convey the hospitality and kindness shown to me in South Africa – or the valued friendships formed. One acknowledgment is especially due. Over the years since our first meeting, the generosity of Nicholas and Liz Ellenbogen has been overwhelming and their boost to the spirit enriching. To them, I tender my deep and affectionate gratitude.

Stewart Conn
Edinburgh – June 1994

POETRY BY STEWART CONN

Thunder in the Air: Akros Publication
The Chinese Tower: Macdonald
Stoats in the Sunlight: Hutchinson
An Ear to the Ground: Hutchinson
Under the Ice: Hutchinson
In the Kibble Palace/New & Selected Poems: Bloodaxe
The Luncheon of the Boating Party: Bloodaxe

Stewart Conn was born in Glasgow in 1936 and brought up in Ayrshire, a dairy-farming county on Scotland's west coast. Married with two sons, he now lives in Edinburgh.

His plays have been staged at home and abroad – most recently in America and Paris. BY THE POOL, set in a suburb of Johannesburg, was first seen on the Edinburgh Festival Fringe in 1988, and given its American premiere at Cleveland Play House, Ohio, in 1991. His work has also been televised and broadcast. In his radio version of Alan Paton's TOO LATE THE PHALAROPE, the central role was movingly played by Yvonne Bryceland.

Of his collections of poems AN EAR TO THE GROUND [1972] was a Poetry Book Society Choice; while other volumes, including UNDER THE ICE [1978], have won Scottish Arts Council awards. Most recent are IN THE KIBBLE PALACE: NEW & SELECTED POEMS [1987] and THE LUNCHEON OF THE BOATING PARTY [1992] (both published by Bloodaxe Books). He is widely anthologised, and has read selections from his work on The Living Poet (BBC Radio 3) and The Poet Speaks (Radio South Africa).

CONTENTS

ARRIVAL, RIVONIA

My room overlooks an oval pool, lit from below.
Between one and the other, trelliswork of vine.
Such the drought, the perimeter a dust-track.
Lemon and pomegranate trees. On the verandah
azure-necked peacocks strut and squawk.

On my first day I am taken to Melrose House,
site of the signing of the Treaty of 1902.
These Kitchener's quarters. I picture his rigid frame
and incongruous round him, a ring of pretty
officers with butterfly-nets cavorting on the lawn.

The jacarandas have no bloom, being out of season.
On the return journey, the car picking up speed,
we pass brightly clad Blacks in the backs of vans
or at bus-stops, lying back in what shade there is.
Otherwise they only occasionally impinge – as when

heading for the theatre in Johannesburg
we swerve to avoid a black youth, another
prancing round him with a knife.
In the wing-mirror, I see them rock together
as though caught in an irresistible slipstream.

Meanwhile the parasols on the verandah
fade in the sun to a uniform pastel.
Distant barking of dogs; a reminder that the world
still spins. Was this once jungle? I turn,
half fearing to find some creature savaged in the pool.

HILLCREST
Alan Paton 1903-88

Having driven through the Valley of a Thousand Hills
I arrive early for my appointment. "He's over eighty,
you must remember; and to conserve his energy,
needs an afternoon nap. So please, not before
three". In the shaded driveway I ponder the irony

of this formerly daring liberal, accused
by his own kind of betraying his birthright,
now so estranged from events; advocacy
of moderation seen as mealy-mouthed by those
to whom brute force, blood-letting the only way.

The purpose of my visit: to deliver
a dramatisation of one of his novels;
and on behalf of a prison-governor,
an admirer over the years, to shake by the hand
the ex-principal of Diepkloof Reformatory.

Behind a vast desk, this flatulent old man. Beside
his typewriter a sheet with: "This is the second
~~and I hope final~~ volume of my autobiography...".
The conversation of Glasgow, his father's home;
this land he loves; conscience and expediency.

Leaving I recall his "Kontakion for You, Departed",
after Plato, purifying as anything I've read.
In frailness even, illumined among the acacias
like an allegorical figure, his precept first and last:
To punish and not restore, the greatest of all offences.

SIGHTS AND SOUNDS
for Sue Clark

From my Cape Town hotel, an incessant
barking of dogs; in the Malay Quarter
the muezzin's interminable wail.
I twitch the curtain: a cockroach scuttles.
The preposterous sun splits Signal Hill.

Soon on the car radio, the mellifluous tones
of the English Service tell of the release
on Robben Island of an undisclosed number
of penguins; heavy news, in Afrikaans;
and on Springbok, "the Rise and Shine Show,

setting you on your way, this Wednesday".
Past the Hospital Bend intersection
where the accident rate, many years ago,
dropped temporarily with the installation
of a sign, "Dr. Barnard is waiting for you".

Domains fragrant with thyme and rosemary;
then Groot Constantia, balm to the eye,
its facade exquisite as sugar-ice
against an azure sky. All porcelain
and honeyed furniture. Upstairs, a clutter

of Edwardiana: old 78's, gramophones
with the original horns. Tempting
to put them on, throw open the windows
and let loose a cacophony ranging from
"Now is the hour" to "Excerpts from *Lohengrin*".

GOOD HOPE

The frontage of Cape Town's Lutheran
Church, of elegant proportion,

will occupy the memory
more than architecturally.

Separateness witnessed to a degree
beyond anything I thought I'd see

I still encounter hope, a bright
light at almost dead of night.

In this a similarity
to Luther's finest quality:

were the world to end tomorrow, he
still would plant his apple tree.

OUTSIDER
to Jeremy Cronin

Reading the poems you gave me, I marvel
at a resolution beyond my comprehension,
the lyrical intensity
governing what you have to say.

And face pressed helplessly
against my hotel-room window,
am unable to eradicate
from my mind the glass plate

through which for one quarter
of an hour, on the day
your wife died, you saw her mother
sobbing, and could not comfort her.

                       To what
can one cling, when monstrosity
exists beyond reason?

                 Pigeons beat
their wings and walk heel-toe
on the roof below.

             The Lutheran Church opposite
is tiered like a wedding-cake,
against a dark sky.

        Whose knife is at whose throat?

HOUSE GUEST

I let myself in
and in the gathered gloom,
pour a glass of wine,
and make for the sitting-room

where I become aware
of a clicking
too regular
for twigs against the pane.

Telling myself, too metallic
for snake,
I sidle to the door,
switch the light on.

A caged hamster,
pure white with ruby eyes,
circles ceaselessly
in its treadmill of wire.

DOUBLE EXPOSURE

When I returned from the Shopping Centre on Tuesday afternoon
our next-door neighbour was waiting outside. She'd forgotten
her key, could she come in till her husband got back. All of two
hours, it must've been. He didn't say a thing, just took her
into their house, and proceeded to beat her black and blue.

Yesterday as I was watering the garden a passer-by called out
that a dog was caught in next-door's gate. It was our Doberman,
eyes popping from her head, neck stretched like a chicken.
She must've climbed over and been attacked by their Rottweiler.
Trapped trying to escape, she was slowly strangling in the wire.

I shouted to my neighbour, watching from her porch, to open it.
"Your dog has no right to be there" she replied, going indoors.
The passer-by and I clawed at the mesh until our fingers tore,
eventually releasing it. I drove with the dog to the vet,
who said only a few more minutes, and she would have had it.

He stitched her up as best he could. Now she can't go out.
Last night all I could do was concentrate on TV,
trying not to think of those Afrikaners next door
and how often you hear, of violence in our country,
"Those bloody Blacks, always at each other's throats!"

SOWETO PHOTOGRAPHS
for Bernard Spong and Rykie Woite

i

Entering Soweto, we pull up to photograph
the contrasting sides of the street: huts
of corroded metal, opposite shacks even older,
squatting in their own detritus. Half
naked children play among rubber tyres.
A dog grapples with a hoop of wire.

A car draws in: a plainclothes patrolman
in shirt and slacks, gun-butt showing.
He asks the driver's occupation.
"Minister of religion... my friend
from abroad is keen to see round."
He gestures dismissively. We drive on.

ii

Outside the United Congregational
pre-school nursery, twenty children
by means of a plastic mickey-mouse
are taught the words for different colours
in a language not their own. When they get over
the novelty of my presence, I take my pictures

then saunter self-consciously to the street.
There screeches up a van, from which dangle
men in balaclavas: they leap off, empty
dust-bins, are on again and away.
A coalman reins up, wets his eyebrows
and poses as if to say, *Take me, Take me...*

iii

"Down there, all that remains of
Sophiatown... remember Huddleston,
the bulldozing?" Smoke obscures the sun.
Next, Tutu's house: the brave one.
And on, and on. Soon we approach
Orlando Stadium for which

in '76, the children were heading.
My guide saw the bodies lying,
bullets in their back. For the anniversary
next month, police will congregate
on this waste ground, truncheons
and canisters of tear-gas at the ready.

iv

The faces of the elderly,
runnelled as by long drought;
children caught between one moment
and what the next may bring –
hard to believe these photos
are of the Soweto I saw:

squalid browns, even the brick latrines
picturesque in a way that lessens
their power to horrify, defusing
the rage that should augment
pity. What, I ask my companion,
does one do? "*What little one can.*"

v

Last, a child in a blue tee-shirt,
the lower part of his body bare.
In this light the side of his head
seems cropped. He stares
gravely as I peer
at him, get him in focus...

Now he is on my study wall,
where I tilt at meaningless
windmills, far from his hell.
Huge-eyed, he touches the heart.
Meanwhile, in another murderous
dawn, the world prises itself apart.

STOP-OVER IN BOTSWANA

i

A deluge at Mafeking – first rain
for two years. Each intersection
a mud ravine. Food-stalls open,
the museum closed for Saturday afternoon.
I bolt a portion of chicken, move on.

No longer the limitless grainlands
of Western Transvaal, rich farms like bulwarks,
filling-stations a dependable distance between.
Scrub. Vans laden with soaked workmen.
Bophuthatswana. Terrain of orange and green.

A black boy I give a lift to
beckons to be set down. The next
points at the sky. "More to come."
The rainbow's end, in a shanty
suburb, ever more illusory.

Soon the outskirts of Gaborone.
The rainbow double now, and full.
Darkness falling I phone
from the disdainful President Hotel
the friend of a friend with whom

I am to stop over. Allocated "the room"
I wake before dawn. Above my head,
squashed shapes. Mosquitos, I assume.
Till one is hard to the touch.
The light on: gobbets of chewing-gum.

ii

Next day in the township of Oodi,
seated on roasting rock, I wait
for the weavers' co-operative
to open. A maze of mud huts, roofed
with corrugated iron. Beauty in desolation.

A tinkle of goat-bells is obscured
by a passing congregation. Cries of joy.
The leaders in white; the others
a merging in the clear distance
of, it seems, all the colours of the rainbow.

Wall-hangings bought, I wave goodbye
and drive to the compound gate
to find it locked. The weavers have gone.
No-one in sight, I sense eyes everywhere;
was never so conscious of being white.

I retrace my steps, explain. No problem;
just a matter of keeping the goats out.
But the feeling lingers, that night
at a Kalahari concert, the din
insuperable, Masekela on flugelhorn

amplified to such an extent
it's impossible, seated in an alcove
with two poets I've just met,
to yell other than, "Talk later."
The rainbow's arc is hammered into sound.

iii

Early morning, in Gaborone. Familiar
sounds assume a resonance of their own.
Distant dogs howl. Cocks crow,
presaging a dawn it is hard,
in such darkness, to believe will come.

Leaving by way of Lobatsi,
and east. At the border a man
cracks a hide whip at an imaginary
victim; and the Toyota in front of me,
hitting a mirage-patch, rides on air.

Beyond Rustenburg I book in
(having let attractive Swartruggens slip by)
to an unsavoury hotel where instantly
I become another brand of alien:
an *Engelsman* at the heart of Afrikanerdom.

So Botswana recedes in the memory,
comprising part of what supplants it –
itself to be supplanted in turn
by the evolving pattern of the whole.
In a morgue-like hotel bedroom

I shrink at the pounding roar
from a shunting-yard; not the din
but the brute force it manifests;
and an awareness, the cocks still crowing,
of the imminence of that savage dawn.

GOVERNANCE

Sir George Grey, the "perfect Governor":
colonisation seen as a civilising force,
a merging of idealism and the mailed fist.

Determined to clamp down on barbarism
yet not succumb to the excesses of imperialism
he assigned unruly Chiefs to Robben Island

but as part of his grand strategy planned
their sons' and daughters' education.
His vision, harmony amongst races,

collaboration for mutual defence:
this in the mid-nineteenth century.
Were he to regard South Africa today,

certain he would hail the eminence –
violence advocated, the price paid –
of a Prince of the Tembu Royal House.

INTERIOR

The tent resisting the night's chill,
I lie dreaming of giraffe and zebra,
kudu and princely sable. Above all
last night's elephant at the water-hole,
bearing the spirits of his ancestors.

Now the canvas panels glow: blue,
red and white – a cubed drapeau;
then to the howl of whirled
acacia, transporting the spirit,
as in a box-kite, high over Africa.

PILANESBERG

The thornveld is shielded from outside
by a raised lava rim; our camp, within

the stone circle of an Iron Age site.
Inside that, a ring of expended ash:

a dead trampoline – the world's navel.
Morning and night, all snake-fang.

But now an approaching whirlwind
sucks spirals of dust through the air.

No escape, should its crazy zigzag
turn our tamed beast to cavortings of fire.

FLOWERS

Sickle plant

Extravagantly dispersing its reds and yellows
the sickle-plant, offering reassurance at last
to the bottle-brush tree opposite, announces
an imminent end to the long dry season.

For days we wait. Lips parched. The small nerves
at the corners of our mouths twitching slightly,
then uncontrollably. Such the heat's intensity
we realise water, when it does come, may be too late.

Strelitzia

In sharp focus it has the impact of an exotic bird
at rest, so boldly contrasted its primary array
of colour, the confidence of its tail-sheath;
what might be mandibles, curved and scarlet-tipped.

To my eyes, a marvel. But on reporting back
I hear that, in a suburban living-room,
it is thought brash, treated with disdain:
to the *aficionado,* common as Smith, or Mofokeng.

LEOPARD

We stop with a jolt. Scarcely thirty feet away,
a dapple of light becomes a leopard in a fig-tree;
hind legs dangling, rosettes orange and russet.

So insouciant his descent. All muscular nonchalance,
he flows straight for us. Stops, and stares.
We absorb the amber of those wondrous eyes. Last

night's kill guzzled, he scrapes bloodstained grass.
Is gone. Such masterful grace. The stench of entrails
a merciful reminder we are observers, not participants.

AT THE AVIARY

i

An opportunity to observe close-up
those exotics I've been peering at
through binoculars, this past week:
the paradise fly-catcher, long tail
unmistakable; loerie with beaded eye;
most delicate, the lilac-breasted roller.
While I puzzle how to translate them
into print, a precocious bee-eater
settles on my pencil, as though
urging a place be found for him, too.

ii

I stalk a crimson-breasted shrike,
willing him to come my way. Suddenly
he is in front of me, all neck-quirk.
I zoom in as he hops closer, a blur
in the lens. Finally miss out altogether.
A perfect opportunity for observation
muffed through misapplied technique,
I have to go trawling the bird book
for the finer points. But first sheepishly
unfold my checklist, add another tick.

iii

Beyond the inner circle of ibis and egret,
a marabou stork who has lost all dignity.
Little more than a scrag of tatters
on a pole, he displays life's scars;
his once sleek jacket now a filthy misfit.
Pocked by puncture-marks, he is patently
an embarrassment. What they are saying,
conscience tells me, is "Get out of it,
and take your cardboard box with you,
before you further lower the tone of the place".

ON THE WATER

i

Two warblers nestmaking in the reeds
commute like inverted arrows,
a series of bobs and flounces,
as if stitching a tapestry, or fixing
pegs on an invisible clothes-line.
Meanwhile the weavers, those wise
virgins, flit from their upside-down
domains and hurtle like lightning
into dense acacia-clumps – without
ever impaling themselves on the spikes.

ii

An irascible hornbill casts
a jaundiced eye, can't quite
credit it, so casts another.
Extends head and neck upwards,
to emit vertical streamers
of sound. Another responds,
close by – distance an irrelevance:
like Italian tenors, supposedly
addressing one another, but in reality,
each playing to the back of the house.

iii

Nesting marabou observe with an hauteur
ill becoming their role of scavengers,
unable to take in that far from the main
attraction, they merely occupy boxes
on the periphery of the action. Fly-catchers
and bee-eaters irradiate the air. The jacana
even, stilting across the water-lilies,
no more than the supporting *corps-de-ballet*
for a purple gallinule performing almost faster
than the eye can take in, *entrechat* upon *entrechat*.

JEDIBE CAMP

Trust

Spiky umbels of papyrus bob against my face
as Trust, the head poler, steers through
channels scarcely wide enough to take us.
Reaching an island of baobab, Trust places

a finger to his lips, points at a silhouette
bunched high on a fork: a Pels fishing owl.
I can just pick it out – a blotch of cinnamon
and white. Trust gives the thumbs-up.

Poling the mokoro back across the lagoon
he says he hopes his son will go to school
(as he didn't) and learn to read and write
(which his father did, in the diamond mine).

He names the water-birds in his own tongue
and Latin; showing no bitterness
at working, after deductions for food
and board, for a miserly daily rate.

Next day on the plane, I'll find myself seated
behind a lady who "came all the way from Minnesota
just to see the Pels: worth every cent, believe me":
member of neither a rare nor an endangered species.

Water Two

Our boat moored to the reeds, Water Two
catches three tiger-fish, myself none.
Nor the elderly Zimbabwean in the bow.
Suddenly at 7 a.m., we are into a shoal

of barbel. After three revolutions
my reel screams, then slackens –
the leader bitten through. I land a bream.
The mozzies take over. "Tiger next time!"

Alongside our catch, on the grass,
instead of the customary fly-box
the size 6 shoe of a former Miss South Africa
here on a promotional tour. In the small hours

I think of her stretching those lissom limbs;
while in the next tent the Zimbabwean
laments Mugabe's latest sequestrations.
Hourly, the snuffle of hippo

in the surrounding swamp. Already, Okavango
a jewel, in the brain. After coffee and fruit,
I find my backpack speckled with birdshit.
The previous day's catch, fish-eagle bait.

Over the Desert

Entering the Kalahari the pure waters
of the Delta, rather than form an estuary,
peter out in a depth of sand so great
even major earth tremors leave no trace

but are absorbed before reaching the surface.
Subjecting our lives, scarcely
more substantial, to varied analogy:
refreshment, or drought, of the spirit;

placing ourselves at others'
disposal; from this, to loss
of enlightenment over the centuries.
Below, a terrain *in extremis*,

dry valleys and fossil dunes
extending to the horizon and beyond;
the world's curve, billions of sandgrains.
Through a blur of condensation

imagine mirage-like, hazy and wavery,
an ancient Bushman and his wife, alone
in the thornveld, awaiting the hyenas
through whom they will join their ancestors.

THE SURVIVORS

The ostrich, our biggest bird, unable
to fly, presents a plumed posterior
to spear or twelve-bore. Grown
accustomed to depiction as the cliché'd
opter-out, classic burier of head
in sand, it has down the years
been a prime candidate for extinction.

My first encounter in a nature reserve:
a battery of lenses poked from parked cars
withdrawn, windows wound up hastily,
as a row of sinewy fluffballs
extend scrawny necks, hungrily. Later
in the bushveld, a rival pair of males
kick-start, reveal formidable power.

More recently, men racing one another
on ostrich-back, clear that while graceless,
such speed and muscularity reduce
their riders to something lesser.
Instilled further, in themselves
as survivors: a confidence
they will one day come into their own.